Pineapple Chunks to Bittersweet Chocolate and Cashew Sl[...] Other treats include Almon[...] Coffee Frozen Yogurt Sandwiches, Pomegranate [...] Vanilla Bean Frozen Yogurt [...] Chunky Banana Flax Semifreddo.

All the Chilled Desserts are gluten-free (and often raw) and include Cacao Pecan Bars with Creamy Avocado Frosting, Mojito Mousse on Coconut Crunch and Lemon Cashew Bars.

Finally [...] ously [...] th

Choosing healthier foods can still mean satisfying your soul whilst nourishing your body. These recipes from your friends at SNOG will inspire you to prepare treats that you will love but that will also love you back!

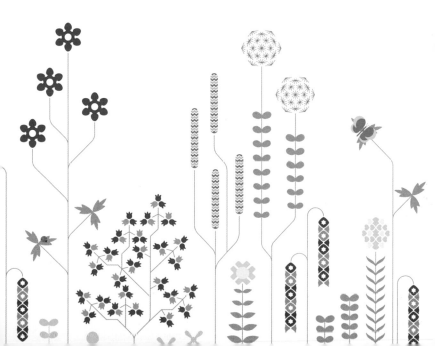

frozen
yogurt

frozen yogurt

and other cool recipes
for healthy treats

SNOG™

RYLAND PETERS & SMALL
LONDON • NEW YORK

This book is dedicated to the pursuit of healthy eating and encouraging our physical, mental and spiritual well-being.

Recipe Developers and Writers
Mariana Velasquez and Cristina Archila

Photography Kate Whitaker

Original Design, Photographic Art Direction and Prop Styling
Steve Painter

Designer Emily Breen

Production Controller Mai-Ling Collyer

Art Director Leslie Harrington

Editorial Director Julia Charles

Publisher Cindy Richards

Food Stylist Lucy McKelvie

Illustrator Akira Chatani

Indexer Hilary Bird

Snog corporate branding and company graphic design ICO Design

First published in 2011
This revised edition published in 2019
by Ryland Peters & Small
20–21 Jockey's Fields
London WC1R 4BW
and
341 east 116th Street
New York, NY 10029

10 9 8 7 6 5 4 3 2 1

Recipes featured in this book were originally published in The Snog Healthy Treats Cookbook in 2011

Text © Pablo Uribe 2011, 2019
Design and photography
© Ryland Peters & Small 2011, 2019

Printed in China

ISBN: 978-1-78879-088-8

A CIP record for this book is available from the British Library.

US Library of Congress cataloging-in-publication data has been applied for.

Important note about the recipes
• For best results we recommend using an ice cream maker for the frozen yogurt recipes in this book.
• All spoon measurements are level, unless otherwise specified.
• When a recipe calls for the grated zest/peel of citrus fruit, buy unwaxed fruit and wash it well before using.

contents

why eat Snog healthy treats?

Making the 'best' choice is crucial when it comes to eating sweet treats. Most of us love them; they are a celebration of life. Treats are a special delight; they should nourish our body and satisfy our soul. Choosing healthy treats will benefit our organs, our mind and our planet.

When we eat wholesome, fresh ingredients, our bodies become leaner, our skin glows and our energy levels increase. Our whole lifestyle shifts and ultimately becomes healthier. These food choices are powerful decisions that dictate what we look like and how we feel. Taking responsibility for how we nourish ourselves goes far beyond food; it's who we are and it's how we relate to the planet.

Ultimately, if food keeps us alive, shouldn't we consume lively foods? Lively foods are whole, natural foods that contain valuable nutrients and support sustainability. As we consume these foods we enable our bodies to assimilate more nutrients and eliminate proper waste. Our bodies understand the composition of whole, natural foods and benefit from them when eaten in balanced amounts. The closer an ingredient remains to its pure and natural form, the more beneficial it will be for all of us. Ultimately, the origin, handling and quality of our food matters a great deal. It is our own responsibility to relate to the food we eat with greater consciousness. We need to stay informed about healthy and sustainable options. Choosing healthier foods should not mean sacrificing flavour in any way. It may mean exploring, planning or preparing foods with a bit more diligence, but that's a small task in return for optimal health, well-being and longevity.

This shift towards a healthier lifestyle will expand awareness in many aspects of our lives. Inevitably we develop interest in the stories behind our food, its origins and how it affects all of us. It becomes clear why we need to treat food with greater significance. It is our very own preventive medicine and it dictates the quality of our life. It is our vital energy source and we have the privilege of making the 'best' possible choice every time.

May the recipes in this book inspire you to get adventurous and prepare many delicious healthy treats – food that we love and that loves us back.

frozen
treats

Snog pure frozen yogurt

We developed these recipes for the home, looking to achieve the tangy, fresh and clean-tasting qualities of our frozen yogurt by using some of the same basic natural ingredients. At our shops we use specialized commercial equipment that imparts the right amount of air and maintains the perfect temperature for smoothness.

720 ml / 3 cups plain Greek yogurt (0% fat)

360 ml / 1½ cups organic low-fat milk

120 ml / ½ cup agave nectar

2 teaspoons freshly squeezed lemon juice

an ice cream maker (optional)

Makes about 1.4 litres / 1.5 quarts

natural

Whisk together the yogurt, milk, agave nectar and lemon juice in a large bowl. Transfer to the bowl of an ice cream maker and churn according to the manufacturer's directions, until creamy and smooth. If you do not have an ice cream maker, pour the mixture into a freezerproof container, put on the lid and place in the freezer. After about 45 minutes check the mixture. As it starts to freeze around the edges, beat vigorously with a fork, whisk, electric hand-held mixer or spatula to break up the ice crystals. Repeat periodically until the mixture is frozen, about 2–3 hours.

chocolate

Follow the recipe for Natural Pure Frozen Yogurt (see above), whisking in 3 tablespoons of sifted good-quality unsweetened cocoa powder (ideally Italian) before freezing.

green tea

Follow the recipe for Natural Pure Frozen Yogurt (see above), whisking in 1 tablespoon of green matcha tea powder before freezing.

pomegranate vanilla bean frozen yogurt

Pomegranate molasses is a great ingredient. It contains no added sugar and its flavour is strong and sharp. A little goes a long way and it's perfect for drizzling.

120 ml / ½ cup organic low-fat milk

1 vanilla pod/bean

180 ml / ¾ cup unsweetened pomegranate juice

840 ml / 3½ cups plain Greek yogurt (0% fat)

160 ml / ⅔ cup agave nectar

2 tablespoons pomegranate molasses

pomegranate drizzle (optional)

480 ml / 2 cups pomegranate juice

an ice cream maker (optional)

Makes about 1 litre / quart

Put the milk in a pan over medium heat. Split the vanilla pod/bean in half lengthways and scrape the seeds into the milk. Add the pod/bean. Bring the milk to a simmer, cover and remove from the heat. Let stand for 10–15 minutes to infuse. Remove the pod/bean and allow the milk to cool.

Put the pomegranate juice, yogurt, agave nectar and pomegranate molasses in a large bowl. Stir in the infused milk. Refrigerate until cold.

Transfer to the bowl of an ice cream maker and churn according to the manufacturer's directions, until creamy and smooth. If you do not have an ice cream maker, pour the mixture into a freezerproof container, put on the lid and place in the freezer. After about 45 minutes check the mixture. As it starts to freeze around the edges, beat vigorously with a fork, whisk, electric hand-held mixer or spatula to break up the ice crystals. Repeat periodically until the mixture is frozen, about 2–3 hours.

To make the pomegranate drizzle, put the pomegranate juice in a pan over medium/high heat. Bring to the boil then reduce the heat to medium/low. Simmer for 35 minutes or until reduced to about 120 ml / ½ cup. Chill and drizzle over the frozen yogurt to serve.

apricot cardamom frozen yogurt with pistachio swirl

Fresh apricots are a delicious summer treat and using them in all ways possible is a must! Here the exotic Middle Eastern flavours of cardamom and pistachios evoke a Persian garden in bloom.

360 ml / 1½ cups vanilla-flavoured low-fat yogurt

240 ml / 1 cup fat-free buttermilk

120 ml / ½ cup apricot nectar (see note on page 58)

1 tablespoon freshly squeezed lemon juice

140 g / ¾ cup diced fresh apricots

60 ml / ¼ cup agave nectar

⅛ teaspoon ground cardamom (alternatively use 2–3 cardamom pods, split them, scoop out the seeds and crush finely)

3 tablespoons chopped toasted pistachios

an ice cream maker (optional)

Makes 1.4 litres / 1.5 quarts

Put the yogurt, buttermilk, apricot nectar, lemon juice and apricots in a large bowl and stir to combine. Transfer the mixture to the bowl of an ice cream maker and churn according to the manufacturer's directions, until creamy and smooth. If you do not have an ice cream maker, pour the mixture into a freezerproof container, put on the lid and place in the freezer. After about 45 minutes check the mixture. As it starts to freeze around the edges, beat vigorously with a fork, whisk, electric hand-held mixer or spatula to break up the ice crystals. Repeat periodically until the mixture is frozen, about 4 hours.

Stir together the agave nectar and cardamom powder or crushed cardamom seeds in a small bowl and set aside.

Take the frozen yogurt out of the freezer and allow it to soften slightly. Sprinkle the toasted pistachios over the top and pour the agave nectar and cardamom mixture into the frozen yogurt. Using a rubber spatula, make a few strokes to partially mix it in, then return to the freezer until ready to serve.

lemongrass basil frozen yogurt

In Vietnamese cuisine, fresh herbs give the spicy, rich food a remarkable lightness. Inspired by dishes where lemongrass delicately envelopes rich flavours, this recipe combines aromatic herbs with creamy frozen yogurt.

4 thin lemongrass stalks, washed and roughly chopped

180 ml / ¾ cup agave nectar

570 g / 2½ cups plain Greek yogurt (0% fat)

180 ml / ¾ cup organic low-fat milk

½ teaspoon finely grated lime zest

2 tablespoons freshly squeezed lime juice

2 tablespoons thinly shredded fresh purple Thai basil (or ordinary basil if unavailable)

an ice cream maker (optional)

Makes 1.4 litres / 1.5 quarts

Put the lemongrass and agave nectar in a small saucepan set over medium/high heat. Bring to the boil and cook for 3–4 minutes, until the mixture becomes bubbly white. Remove from the heat and allow to sit for a further 5 minutes so that the lemongrass taste infuses the agave nectar. Strain through a sieve/strainer to remove the lemongrass and set the nectar aside. Allow to cool completely.

Put the yogurt, milk, lime zest and lime juice in large bowl. Stir to combine. Pour in the lemongrass-scented agave nectar and add the basil. Stir well. Refrigerate the mixture until very cold.

Transfer to the bowl of an ice cream maker and churn according to the manufacturer's directions, until creamy and smooth. If you do not have an ice cream maker, pour the mixture into a freezerproof container, put on the lid and place in the freezer. After about 45 minutes check the mixture. As it starts to freeze around the edges, beat vigorously with a fork, whisk, electric hand-held mixer or spatula to break up the ice crystals. Repeat periodically until the mixture is frozen, about 2–3 hours. Serve in scoops.

lemon lavender frozen yogurt

If you come across Meyer lemons, usually in season around January, do not hesitate to use them in this recipe. The exquisite tangy yet floral taste of this delicious frozen yogurt is sure to impress.

720 ml / 3 cups plain Greek yogurt (0% fat)

2 tablespoons finely grated lemon zest

120 ml / ½ cup freshly squeezed lemon juice

180 ml / ¾ cup organic wild flower honey

1 tablespoon fresh lavender sprigs or ¼ teaspoon dried lavender

an ice cream maker (optional)

Makes 1.4 litres / 1.5 quarts

Put the yogurt, lemon zest and lemon juice in a large bowl. Stir to combine.

Heat the honey and lavender in a small saucepan set over medium heat, until you can smell the lavender's scent. Strain through a fine sieve/strainer and allow to cool completely. Discard the lavender.

Add the lavender-infused honey to the yogurt and lemon juice mixture, and stir to combine.

Transfer to the bowl of an ice cream maker and churn according to the manufacturer's directions, until creamy and smooth. If you do not have an ice cream maker, pour the mixture into a freezerproof container, put on the lid and place in the freezer. After about 45 minutes check the mixture. As it starts to freeze around the edges, beat vigorously with a fork, whisk, electric hand-held mixer or spatula to break up the ice crystals. Repeat periodically until the mixture is frozen, about 2–3 hours. Serve in small scoops.

almond coffee frozen yogurt sandwiches

This chilly treat is a wonderful 'caffeine quencher' afternoon snack on a hot day, as well as being an impressive dessert.

almond cookies

4 egg whites

275 g / 3 ½ cups flaked/ slivered almonds

120 ml / ½ cup agave nectar

½ teaspoon pure vanilla extract

¼ teaspoon sea salt

coffee frozen yogurt

720 ml / 3 cups plain Greek yogurt (0% fat)

360 ml / 1 ½ cups organic fat-free milk

120 ml / ½ cup agave nectar

2 tablespoons Italian instant espresso powder

2 teaspoons freshly squeezed lemon juice

an ice cream maker (optional)

2 large baking sheets, greased and lined with baking parchment, also greased and dusted with flour

Makes 8

Preheat the oven to 160°C (325°F) Gas 3.

Put the egg whites, almonds, agave nectar, vanilla and salt in a bowl. Stir until combined. Use the back of a spoon to spread 2 tablespoons of the mixture on the baking sheets in 8-cm / 3-inch rounds. Bake for 20–25 minutes, until the edges are golden brown. Let the cookies cool for 10 minutes on the baking sheets, then carefully transfer to a wire rack to cool completely.

Whisk together all the coffee frozen yogurt ingredients in a large bowl. Transfer to the bowl of an ice cream maker and churn according to the manufacturer's directions, until creamy and smooth. If you do not have an ice cream maker, pour the mixture into a freezerproof container, put on the lid and place in the freezer. After about 45 minutes check the mixture. As it starts to freeze around the edges, beat vigorously with a fork, whisk, electric hand-held mixer or spatula to break up the ice crystals. Repeat periodically until the mixture is frozen, about 2–3 hours.

To assemble, spoon 2 tablespoons of coffee frozen yogurt onto half of the cookies. Top with the remaining cookies to make sandwiches. Place in the freezer, but transfer to the refrigerator 20 minutes before serving.

chunky banana flax semifreddo

Semifreddos make great desserts for entertaining as they can be made in advance and simply removed from the freezer, turned out and sliced to serve.

3 egg yolks

400-ml / 13½-oz. can coconut milk

3 bananas, cut into chunks

120 ml / ½ cup agave nectar

2 tablespoons freshly squeezed lemon juice

25 g / ¼ cup chopped macadamia nuts

15 g / ½ oz. good-quality dark/bittersweet chocolate chunks

1 tablespoon ground linseed/flax seed meal

⅛ teaspoon sea salt

a 23 x 13 x 6-cm / 9 x 5 x 2½-inch loaf pan, fully lined with clingfilm/plastic wrap

Serves 6

Put the egg yolks and 120 ml / ½ cup of the coconut milk in a metal bowl set over a saucepan of gently simmering water. Whisk for 6 minutes, until the mixture has doubled in volume. Remove the bowl from the heat and continue whisking until cool.

Purée the bananas, agave nectar, lemon juice and remaining coconut milk in a blender until smooth. Stir into the egg and coconut mixture.

Pour half the mixture into the prepared loaf pan and smooth over the top. Cover loosely with clingfilm/plastic wrap and put in the freezer for 1 hour. Store the remaining banana mixture in the fridge until required.

Remove the loaf pan from the freezer and sprinkle the macadamias, chocolate and ground linseed/flax meal over the top. Pour in the remaining banana mixture, cover loosely with clingfilm/plastic wrap and freeze for at least 4 hours. To serve, turn out onto a platter, remove the clingfilm/plastic wrap and slice.

blackberry chocolate pops

Refreshing and indulgent, these are delicious and a big hit with the kids. The crunchy seeds provide a delicious texture as you bite into the frozen pop. If you like, you can replace the blackberries with raspberries or strawberries.

blackberry mixture

175 g / 1⅓ cups fresh blackberries

4 tablespoons agave nectar

1 teaspoon finely grated lemon zest

2 tablespoons freshly squeezed lemon juice

chocolate mixture

4 tablespoons agave nectar

25 g / ⅓ cup good-quality cocoa powder

1 teaspoon pure vanilla extract

an 8 x 75-g / 3-oz. capacity ice lolly/popsicle mould or similar

8 wooden ice lolly/popsicle sticks

Makes 8

Put the blackberries, agave nectar, lemon zest and lemon juice in the bowl of a food processor or a blender. Add 180 ml / ¾ cup cold water and purée until smooth.

Pour the blackberry mixture into the moulds, filling each one just half way. Freeze for up to 1 hour.

In the meantime prepare the chocolate mixture. Put the agave nectar, cocoa and vanilla in a small saucepan set over medium heat. Add 180 ml / ¾ cup cold water and bring to the boil, whisking continuously until the cocoa dissolves completely. Remove from the heat, let cool then chill thoroughly.

Remove the pops from the freezer and spoon the chocolate mixture into the moulds, on top of the blackberry mixture. Return to the freezer. After 30 minutes remove the pops from the freezer and insert a wooden stick in the centre of each one. Return to the freezer and freeze until completely frozen and firm before serving.

chapter 2

healthy toppings

peanut pineapple chunks

Any excuse to eat sweet and caramelized pineapple is a good excuse. The peanut butter here adds the creamy nutty coating that keeps you craving more.

450 g / 1 lb. fresh pineapple, cubed

70 g / ¼ cup smooth organic peanut butter

60 ml / ¼ cup agave nectar

60 ml / ¼ cup canned tamarind juice

2 tablespoons peanut oil

Snog Pure Frozen Yogurt (see page 9), to serve

a baking sheet, lightly greased

Makes about 500 g/4 cups

Preheat the oven to 190°C (375°F) Gas 5.

Put the pineapple cubes, peanut butter, agave nectar, tamarind juice and oil in a large bowl and mix well to combine and to coat the pineapple chunks fully.

Spread the chunks out onto the prepared baking sheet and bake in the preheated oven for 12–15 minutes, until the edges of the pineapple become dark and crispy and the juices have thickened.

Remove from the oven and allow to cool. Spoon over scoops of your favourite Snog Pure Frozen Yogurt to serve.

The peanut pineapple chunks can be stored in an airtight container in the refrigerator for up to 3 days.

candied rhubarb with strawberries and basil

Here the tangy sweet fruit and fresh basil come together in a delicate and aromatic combination. The rhubarb is marinated overnight so you'll need to plan ahead.

450 g / 2 cups sliced fresh rhubarb

240 ml / 1 cup agave nectar

120 ml / ½ cup white wine

2 strawberry fruit 'tea' bags

230 g / 2 cups sliced fresh strawberries

8 fresh basil leaves, torn

Snog Pure Frozen Yogurt (see page 9), to serve

Serves 4

Put the rhubarb in a heat-resistant bowl. Put the agave nectar and wine in a saucepan set over medium heat and add 240 ml / 1 cup cold water. Bring to the boil and add the strawberry 'tea' bags. Cover and remove from the heat. Let stand for 5 minutes.

Remove the 'tea' bags, bring the liquid back to the boil and then carefully pour it over the sliced rhubarb. Cover tightly with clingfilm/plastic wrap and allow to cool completely. Refrigerate overnight and stir in the strawberries and basil leaves just before serving.

Spoon over scoops of your favourite Snog Pure Frozen Yogurt to serve. This topping is best enjoyed on the day it is made.

roasted summer fruits

Make sure all the fruit you are using is ripe and sweet; nothing is worse than a mealy nectarine or peach. Adding a little wine is a sort of welcome to the upcoming grape harvest, but feel free to replace with unsweetened grape juice, if preferred.

1 large peach, cut into 5-mm / ¼-inch wedges

1 large nectarine, cut into 5-mm / ¼-inch wedges

1 plum, cut into 5-mm / ¼-inch wedges

8 cherries, pitted and halved

4 tablespoons agave nectar

¼ teaspoon freshly ground black pepper

4 tablespoons red wine or 4 tablespoons unsweetened grape juice

Snog Natural Pure Frozen Yogurt (see page 9), to serve

a rimmed baking sheet, lined with baking parchment

Serves 4–6

Preheat the oven to 180°C (350°F) Gas 4.

Put the peach, nectarine and plum slices, along with the cherries, onto the prepared baking sheet.

Put the agave nectar, black pepper and red wine in a small bowl and whisk until combined. Drizzle over the fruit and bake in the preheated oven for 25–30 minutes, until golden, juicy and partially caramelized. Allow the roasted fruit to cool slightly on the baking sheet.

Serve the roasted fruits warm, spooned over generous scoops of Snog Natural Pure Frozen Yogurt.

These roasted fruits will keep stored in an airtight container in the refrigerator for up to 3 days.

cinnamon sweet potatoes with salty pumpkin seeds

Sweet and salty flavours are marvellous when enjoyed together. This unusual topping beautifully enhances the tangy taste of Snog frozen yogurt.

1 sweet potato (about 280 g / 10 oz.) cut into 5-mm / ¼-inch dice

2 tablespoons roasted salted hulled pumpkin seeds (see note)

2 tablespoons sultanas/ golden raisins

¼ teaspoon ground cinnamon

1 tablespoon palm/date sugar or 2 teaspoons agave nectar

2 teaspoons coconut oil

Snog Pure Frozen Yogurt (see page 9), to serve

Serves 4–6

Preheat the oven to 190°C (375°F) Gas 5

Put the sweet potatoes, pumpkin seeds and sultanas/golden raisins on a baking sheet. Sprinkle over the cinnamon and palm/date sugar or agave nectar, drizzle with the coconut oil and stir to coat.

Bake in the preheated oven for about 25 minutes, stirring 2 or 3 times, until evenly roasted and the sweet potatoes are tender and starting to caramelize.

Let cool on the baking sheet for 5 minutes. Serve sprinkled over generous scoops of your favourite Snog Pure Frozen Yogurt.

This topping will keep stored in an airtight container in the refrigerator for up to 2 days.

Note: If you cannot find roasted salted hulled pumpkin seeds, you can make them as follows. Toss some hulled pumpkin seeds lightly in olive oil then put them on a baking sheet and sprinkle with sea salt. Bake in an oven preheated to 150°C (300°F) Gas 2 for about 30–40 minutes, stirring every 10 minutes, until roasted.

bittersweet chocolate and cashew slivers

This summery mixture of dried fruits and nuts works beautifully but you can try any combination you like, such as dried pineapple and pistachios or raisins and almonds. Although the cacao nibs are optional, they do add a wonderful crunch to every bite.

225 g / 8 oz. good-quality dark/bittersweet chocolate (70% cocoa solids), chopped

2 teaspoons agave nectar

60 g / ½ cup roasted cashew nuts

45 g / ¼ cup dried blueberries

45 g / ¼ cup dried nectarines, chopped

1 tablespoon cacao nibs (optional)

Snog Pure Frozen Yogurt (see page 9), to serve

a baking sheet, lined with baking parchment

Serves 8

Put the chocolate in a heat-resistant bowl set over a saucepan of gently simmering water. Do not let the base of the bowl touch the water. Stir continuously until melted.

Remove from the heat and stir in the agave nectar. Pour onto the prepared baking sheet. Spread out using the back of a metal spoon or a metal spatula and sprinkle liberally with the cashews, dried fruit and cacao nibs, if using.

Allow to cool on the baking sheet at room temperature for 2–3 hours, until hard. Break into large shards and serve with generous scoops of your favourite Snog Pure Frozen Yogurt.

These slivers will keep stored in an airtight container in a cool place for up to 3 days.

pomegranate, white chocolate and peppermint mix

Pomegranate seeds could be described as tangy sweet jewels. The subtle taste of white chocolate and the intense aroma of natural peppermint contrast with the seeds here to create a combination sublime in both texture and taste.

120 g / 1 cup toasted walnuts, roughly chopped

100 g / ½ cup good-quality white chocolate chunks

2 tablespoons small fresh peppermint leaves

80 g / ½ cup pomegranate seeds

1 tablespoon pomegranate molasses

Snog Pure Frozen Yogurt (see page 9), to serve

Serves 6–8

Combine the walnuts, chocolate chunks, peppermint leaves and pomegranate seeds in a small bowl. Add the pomegranate molasses and stir well to coat all of the ingredients.

Serve the mix sprinkled over generous scoops of your favourite Snog Pure Frozen Yogurt.

This topping will keep stored in an airtight container in the refrigerator for 2–3 days.

blueberry, ginger and lemon sauce

A fragrant sauce that calls to mind the summery scent of fresh berries and the soothing qualities of ginger.

400 g / 3 cups fresh blueberries

1 tablespoon finely grated lemon zest

60 ml / ¼ cup freshly squeezed lemon juice

3 tablespoons agave nectar

2 tablespoons finely grated fresh ginger

Snog Pure Frozen Yogurt (see page 9), to serve

Serves 8

Put the blueberries, lemon zest, lemon juice, agave nectar and ginger in the bowl of a food processor or a blender and purée until very smooth.

Spoon over scoops of your favourite Snog Pure Frozen Yogurt to serve.

The sauce can be stored in an airtight container in the refrigerator for up to 3 days.

crushed dates and figs with cherries and spice

Allspice is a complex ingredient, it tastes like cinnamon, nutmeg and cloves blended together, but it is in fact a kind of berry that once dried has this unique aroma. The flavours of dates, dried cherries and orange gives this topping a wintry feel.

80 g / ½ cup sliced pitted Medjool dates

80 g / ½ cup chopped dried figs

40 g / ¼ cup sour cherries

⅛ teaspoon ground allspice

2 teaspoons agave nectar

1 tablespoon coconut or almond oil

1 tablespoon freshly squeezed orange juice

Snog Chocolate Pure Frozen Yogurt (see page 9), to serve

Serves 4

Combine the dates, figs, cherries, allspice, agave nectar, coconut oil and orange juice in a large bowl. Let stand at room temperature for at least 10 minutes, to allow the flavours to mingle.

Serve spooned over generous scoops of Snog Chocolate Pure Frozen Yogurt.

These fruits will keep stored in an airtight container in the refrigerator for up to 3 days.

dried ginger black and white sesame crisps

A classic dessert enjoyed in the Middle East is fresh yogurt served with honey and toasted sesame seeds. It's a beautifully balanced combination that, with the addition of cashews and ginger, is perfect with Snog's Green Tea Frozen Yogurt.

1 egg white

50 g / ½ cup chopped roasted cashew nuts

3 tablespoons toasted white sesame seeds

3 tablespoons black sesame seeds

120 ml / ½ cup agave nectar

2 tablespoons desiccated ginger

25 g / ¼ cup coconut flour

¼ teaspoon sea salt

Snog Green Tea Pure Frozen Yogurt (see page 9), to serve

a baking sheet, lined with baking parchment

Makes 18–20

Preheat the oven to 160°C (325°F) Gas 3.

Lightly whisk the egg white in a large bowl. Add the cashews, white and black sesame seeds, agave nectar, ginger, coconut flour and salt. Stir to combine until all the ingredients come together in a sticky mixture.

Place heaped teaspoonfuls of the mixture on the prepared baking sheet, then flatten to create 5-cm / 2-inch rounds.

Bake in the preheated oven for about 25–30 minutes, until golden and crisp. Allow to cool completely. Serve with generous scoops of Snog Green Tea Pure Frozen Yogurt.

Once cold, these crisps will keep stored in an airtight container for up to 5 days.

chapter 3

chilled
desserts

saffron yogurt parfait

Hand-picked saffron is the most delicate spice in the world.
Here, it gives a perfect flavour and colour to this decadent
yogurt parfait!

¼ teaspoon saffron threads

2 tablespoons hot water

480 ml / 2 cups plain Greek
yogurt (0% or 2% fat)

60 ml / ¼ cup agave
nectar

225 g / 1½ cups raw
pecans

130 g / 5 oz. dried Bing
cherries or other tart
variety

325 g / 2 cups finely cubed
mango

Serves 6–8

Dissolve the saffron threads in the hot
water. Set aside for 1 hour.

Strain through a fine sieve/strainer and
discard the saffron threads. Combine
the saffron-infused water with the
yogurt and agave nectar, mixing
thoroughly. Chill in the refrigerator for
1 hour.

Put the pecans and cherries in the
bowl of a food processor and process
to form coarse crumbs.

Divide half of the mixture between
6–8 serving dishes. Top with a layer of
the saffron yogurt and a layer of fresh
mango. Scatter the remaining
crumble mixture on top and serve
immediately.

Stored separately in airtight containers
in the refrigerator, the saffron yogurt
and pecan crumble will keep for up
to 5 days.

passion fruit orange blossom custard cake

Coconut flour is a fabulous discovery for those looking to make gluten-free foods. The surprise is that it doesn't feel like a substitute, but an enriching ingredient that makes the texture interesting and works as a binder.

2 eggs, separated

180 ml / ¾ cup fat-free buttermilk

60 ml / ¼ cup natural passion fruit juice

½ teaspoon finely grated orange zest

½ teaspoon orange-flower water

¼ teaspoon sea salt

2 tablespoons coconut flour

25 g / ¼ cup chopped toasted pistachios

4 individual ramekins or custard cups, lightly oiled

a deep-sided roasting pan, large enough to take the ramekins

Serves 4

Preheat the oven to 160°C (325°F) Gas 3.

Put the egg yolks, buttermilk, passion fruit juice, orange zest, orange-flower water, salt and coconut flour in a mixing bowl and beat until combined.

Put the egg whites in a spotlessly clean bowl and, using a hand-held electric mixer, whisk on medium speed until frothy. Increase the speed as the whites become foamier. Whisk until soft peaks form.

Fold the egg whites into the passion fruit mixture until combined. Spoon into the prepared ramekins and transfer to the roasting pan. Transfer to the preheated oven and carefully add enough water to come halfway up the sides of the ramekins. Bake for 20–25 minutes, until no longer wobbly and the tops are slightly golden.

Let cool slightly on a wire rack. To serve, either leave in the ramekins or run a knife around the edge of the ramekins and turn the cakes out onto serving plates. Sprinkle with chopped pistachios and serve. Alternatively, cover with clingfilm/plastic wrap and chill until ready to serve. They are best enjoyed on the day they are made.

mojito mousse on coconut crunch

This recipe is inspired by the sweet and refreshing citrus and spearmint flavours in the Cuban Mojito cocktail. It is unusual to have avocado in a dessert, but this is always a popular dish.

coconut crunch

100 g / ¾ cup raw walnuts

100 g / 1⅓ cups desiccated/unsweetened shredded dried coconut

¼ teaspoon sea salt

4 soft Medjool dates, pitted and roughly chopped

1 tablespoon agave nectar

mojito mousse

2 Hass avocados

240 ml / 1 cup freshly squeezed lime juice

180 ml / ¾ cup agave nectar

30 g / 1½ cups fresh spearmint leaves, plus a few extra to decorate

2 tablespoons coconut oil or coconut cream

6 lime slices, to decorate

Serves 6

Put the walnuts, coconut and salt in the bowl of a food processor. Process until finely ground and loose but do not overprocess as nuts can easily become a creamy butter. (It is better to process a little at a time and check for consistency.)

Add the dates and agave nectar, and process until the mixture begins to stick together and form coarse crumbs. Sprinkle the mixture into 6 serving dishes. Press to compact with your fingertips. Chill in the refrigerator for 20 minutes.

To make the mojito mousse, put the avocados, lime juice, agave nectar and spearmint in the bowl of a food processor and process until smooth. You may have to stop and scrape down the sides of the bowl a few times. Add the coconut oil while the motor is running, and process until it is incorporated and very smooth.

Distribute the mousse evenly between the dishes. Cover well with clingfilm/plastic wrap and refrigerate for 3 hours. Decorate with spearmint leaves and a lime slice, and serve chilled.

Covered with clingfilm/plastic wrap and stored in the refrigerator, this dessert will keep for 3 days.

lemon cashew bars

If you like lemon bars you will love this exotic version! These beautiful treats are made from crunchy cashew nuts, chewy raisins and tangy lemons. Pre-soaking the cashew nuts enables them to blend more easily into a creamy topping.

base

225 g / 2 cups raw cashew nuts

¼ teaspoon sea salt

40 g / ¼ cup sultanas/ golden raisins

freshly squeezed juice and grated zest of 1 lemon

2 tablespoons agave nectar

topping

100 g / 1 scant cup raw cashew nuts

80 ml / ⅓ cup freshly squeezed lemon juice

60 ml / ¼ cup agave nectar

¼ teaspoon ground turmeric

2 tablespoons coconut oil or coconut cream

1 teaspoon grated lemon zest, to decorate

a 30 x 10-cm / 12 x 4-inch loose-based tart pan, lined with baking parchment

Serves 6

To make the base, put the cashew nuts and salt in the bowl of a food processor and process until coarsely ground. Add the sultanas/golden raisins, lemon juice, lemon zest and agave nectar, and process until the mixture begins to stick together and form coarse crumbs. Sprinkle the mixture in the prepared pan and distribute loosely. Use the tips of your fingers or a spatula to press down to form a base. Chill in the freezer for 20 minutes.

To make the topping, soak the cashew nuts in 480 ml / 2 cups cold water for at least 3 hours and drain well. Combine the cashew nuts, lemon juice and agave nectar in a blender, and process until smooth. Add the turmeric and blend again. Add the coconut oil and blend thoroughly. Pour the topping over the chilled crust and spread evenly with a spatula.

Freeze for 2 hours and then transfer to the refrigerator. Decorate with lemon zest, cut into slices and serve chilled.

Stored in an airtight container in the refrigerator, these bars will keep for up to 4 days.

cacao pecan bars with creamy frosting

This recipe is for all chocolate lovers, so that they can turn their cravings into good nutrition. Cacao is one of nature's most fantastic superfoods with a high antioxidant value. In this recipe, even the creamy frosting has a healthy surprise!

pecan bars

225 g / 2 cups raw pecans

50 g / ½ cup raw cacao powder or good-quality cocoa powder

⅛ teaspoon sea salt

10 soft Medjool dates, pitted

60 ml / ¼ cup agave nectar

cacao avocado frosting

4 soft Medjool dates, pitted

1 Hass avocado

25 g / ¼ cup raw cacao powder or good-quality cocoa powder

60 ml / ¼ cup agave nectar

30 g / scant ⅓ cup raw pecans, roughly chopped, to decorate

a 30 x 10-cm / 12 x 4-inch loose-based tart pan, lined with baking parchment

Serves 6

To make the bars, put the pecans, cacao powder and salt in the bowl of a food processor. Process until finely ground and loose. Add the dates and agave nectar, and process until the mixture begins to stick together and forms coarse crumbs.

Sprinkle the mixture into the prepared pan and distribute loosely. Press evenly to compact using a spatula. Chill in the refrigerator for 20 minutes.

To make the frosting, cover the dates with cold water and soak for 20 minutes. Drain the dates and put them in the bowl of a food processor along with the avocado, cacao powder and agave nectar, and process until smooth. Stop occasionally to scrape down the sides of the bowl with a spatula and process again until very smooth.

Spread the frosting evenly on top of the pecan bars and scatter with chopped pecans. Refrigerate for 2 hours, then cut into 6 slices and serve chilled.

Stored in an airtight container in the refrigerator, these bars will keep for up to 4 days.

pistachio pineapple yogurt crumble

This recipe is inspired by Pablo's sister Xandi's favourite dessert and is where the whole idea for Snog began. A healthy treat that consists of a nut crumble topped with yogurt and fresh fruit. Imagine the possibilities!

325 g / 13 oz. pineapple, finely diced

175 g / 1¼ cups raspberries

60 ml / ¼ cup agave nectar, plus extra to taste

1 tablespoon finely chopped fresh mint leaves

200 g / 1 cup shelled raw pistachio nuts

¼ teaspoon sea salt

8 soft Medjool dates, pitted

1 teaspoon pure vanilla extract

480 ml / 2 cups plain Greek yogurt (0% or 2% fat)

Serves 6–8

Combine the pineapple, raspberries, agave nectar and mint in a bowl and toss lightly. Cover and allow to marinate for at least 15 minutes.

Put the pistachios and salt in the bowl of a food processor and process lightly. Add the dates, vanilla and 1 tablespoon cold water and process until the mixture begins to stick together to form coarse crumbs. Divide most of the mixture between 6–8 serving dishes and top with the yogurt, followed by the marinated pineapple and raspberry. (Drizzle with extra agave nectar if you prefer a sweeter dessert.) Scatter the remaining crumble mixture over the top and serve.

Stored separately in airtight containers in the refrigerator, the marinated fruit and pistachio crumble will keep for 3 days.

apricot cashew cobbler

This fresh-tasting cobbler will make you fall in love with fresh apricots. The delicate compote spooned over a crunchy cashew nut base is a healthy choice for dessert. You can even enjoy this for breakfast.

base
300 g / 2½ cups raw cashew nuts
¼ teaspoon sea salt
2 tablespoons agave nectar
1 teaspoon pure vanilla extract

apricot compote
9 ripe apricots, pitted
70 g / ½ cup dried apricots
60 ml / ¼ cup agave nectar
1 tablespoon freshly squeezed lemon juice

Serves 6–8

Put the cashews and salt in the bowl of a food processor and chop coarsely. Add the agave nectar and vanilla, and pulse lightly. Transfer to a bowl and chill in the refrigerator for 20 minutes.

Put 6 of the fresh apricots, the dried apricots, agave nectar and lemon juice in the bowl of a food processor, and process until smooth. Slice the remaining 3 fresh apricots.

Divide most of the base mixture between 6–8 serving dishes. Top with the apricot compote and fresh apricot slices. Scatter the remaining cashew mixture on top and serve immediately.

Stored separately in airtight containers in the refrigerator, the apricot compote and cashew nut mixture will keep for 4 days.

mango coconut macadamia torte

This recipe is inspired by the tropical flavours of coconut and mango. The torte is surprisingly moist and it's like a bite of island paradise for coconut lovers.

torte base

250 g / 2 cups shelled macadamia nuts

100 g / 1 cup desiccated/unsweetened shredded dried coconut

¼ teaspoon sea salt

16 soft Medjool dates, pitted and roughly chopped

2 teaspoons pure vanilla extract

mango topping

325 g / 12 oz. peeled and cubed ripe mango, plus extra slices, to decorate

3 tablespoons agave nectar

2 teaspoons powdered soya/soy lecithin

3 tablespoons coconut oil

175 g / 1¼ cups raspberries

a 23-cm / 9-inch springform cake pan

Serves 8–10

Put the macadamias, coconut and salt in the bowl of a food processor, and process until finely ground and loose. Add the dates and vanilla, and process until the mixture begins to stick together and form coarse crumbs. Add 2 tablespoons cold water and process again until well mixed. Transfer the mixture to the cake pan and press to compact with a spatula or back of a large spoon. Chill in the refrigerator for 20 minutes.

Put the cubed mango and agave nectar in a blender and purée until smooth. Add the soya/soy lecithin and process again. Add the coconut oil while the motor is running, and process until the mango mixture is very smooth.

Spread the mango mixture over the chilled torte base, using a spatula to level the surface. Cover with clingfilm/plastic wrap and refrigerate for 4 hours. Decorate with slices of mango and fresh raspberries, and serve chilled.

Covered with clingfilm/plastic wrap in the refrigerator, this torte will keep for 4 days.

cool
drinks

chocolatey blueberry pomegranate smoothie

Pomegranates are not only very good for you, but also a visual delight with their jewel-like seeds. Decorate your drink with a few of these fresh seeds for added colour, if you like.

230 g / 2 cups blueberries

360 ml / 1½ cups plain Greek yogurt (0% fat)

80 ml / ⅓ cup unsweetened pomegranate juice

2 tablespoons good-quality cocoa powder

1 teaspoon agave nectar

2 teaspoons almond butter

300 g / 10 oz. ice cubes, crushed (see note)

extra blueberries or pomegranate seeds, to decorate (optional)

Serves 4

Put the blueberries, yogurt, pomegranate juice, cocoa, agave nectar and almond butter in a blender, and process until puréed and smooth.

Just before serving, add the crushed ice and process again until frothy. Pour into tall glasses, garnish with a few fresh blueberries or pomegranate seeds, if using, and serve immediately.

Note: Most blenders can crush ice. If you have a food processor and not a blender, it may not be possible to crush ice in it; check the manufacturer's instructions. Alternatively you can put the ice cubes in a polythene bag and crush them by hitting them with a rolling pin.

coconut ginger smoothie

There's nothing like this warming and energizing smoothie to get you up and out on a chilly morning. Rich and satisfying, it's great for breakfast on the go or served as a mid-afternoon pick-me-up.

240 ml / 1 cup light coconut milk

240 ml/1 cup plain Greek yogurt (0% fat)

2 bananas, cut into chunks

3 tablespoons agave nectar

3 tablespoons freshly squeezed lime juice

1 tablespoon ginger juice or 15 g / 2 tablespoons peeled and grated fresh ginger

200 g / 7 oz. ice cubes, crushed (see note)

ground ginger or slivers of desiccated ginger, to decorate

Serves 4

Put the coconut milk, yogurt, banana chunks, agave nectar, lime juice and ginger juice or grated ginger in a blender and process until smooth. Add the crushed ice and pulse a few times until frothy.

Pour into 4 glass tumblers and decorate with a light sprinkling of ground ginger or a pinch of desiccated ginger, as preferred, and serve immediately.

Note: Most blenders can crush ice. If you have a food processor and not a blender, it may not be possible to crush ice in it; check the manufacturer's instructions. Alternatively you can put the ice cubes in a polythene bag and crush them by hitting them with a rolling pin.

cranberry lemon 'punch'

This is a refreshing and soothing drink that evokes the 1950s favourite, but minus the cloying sweet syrupy flavour and plus the citrusy and bubbly sorbet.

640 ml / 2⅔ cups
unsweetened cranberry
juice

4 scoops lemon sorbet
(about 40 g / 1½ oz. each)

240 ml / 1 cup soda water
or sparkling mineral water

lemon slices, to decorate

ice cubes, to serve

Serves 4

Fill 4 tall glasses with ice cubes. Divide the cranberry juice between them.

Add one scoop of the lemon sorbet to each glass and top up with soda water. Decorate with lemon slices and serve immediately.

minty raspberry nectarine smoothie

Freshly picked raspberries served with yogurt and freshly picked mint conjures up memories of long childhood summers spent picking and devouring fresh raspberries. Here, the flavours have been combined into a smoothie that also contains the sweetness of ripe nectarines.

120 g / 1 cup frozen raspberries

2 nectarines, pitted and quartered

85 g / 1 cup Snog Natural Pure Frozen Yogurt (see page 9)

480 ml / 2 cups nectarine or apricot nectar (see note)

2 tablespoons finely chopped fresh mint

a few extra raspberries and 4 nectarine slices, to decorate

Serves 4

Put the raspberries, nectarines, frozen yogurt, nectarine or apricot nectar and mint in a blender, and process until puréed and smooth.

Pour into 4 glass tumblers, decorate with raspberries and nectarine slices and serve immediately.

Note: Nectarine or apricot nectar is thicker than the juice and is sold in bottles or cans. It's most often found in health food stores or organic markets, but can also be found in larger supermarkets.

orange 'agua fresca' with beet swirl

Street food is often a great source of inspiration for new flavours. Agua fresca is popular in Mexican street markets – they can be made with dazzling combinations of fruits and flowers in an array of stunning colours. This version combines sweet orange juice and a beautiful beetroot/beet swirl.

1 small red beetroot/beet, washed and trimmed

700 ml / 3 cups freshly squeezed orange juice

1 orange, peeled, sliced, and seeded

60 ml / ¼ cup freshly squeezed lemon juice

4 tablespoons agave nectar

2 tablespoons finely grated orange zest

ice cubes, to serve

Serves 4

Preheat the oven to 200°C (400°F) Gas 6.

Put the beetroot/beet on a square of foil. Wrap and transfer to a baking sheet. Roast in the preheated oven for about 40 minutes, until tender when pierced with a knife. Unwrap and allow to cool.

When the beetroot/beet is cold enough to handle, remove the outer skin, cut the flesh into small pieces and set aside.

Put the orange juice, orange slices, lemon juice and 3 tablespoons of the agave nectar in a blender. Add 360 ml / 1½ cups cold water, and process until puréed and smooth.

Chill the orange blend in the refrigerator until very cold. Put the chopped beetroot in a blender with the orange zest, remaining agave nectar and 120 ml / ½ cup cold water, and process until smooth.

To serve, pour the orange agua fresca into 4 tall ice-filled glasses and spoon 1 tablespoon of the beetroot/beet purée on top of each drink. Serve immediately.

papaya lassi

A classic lassi is a delicious sweet-savoury drink made from yogurt and fruit. The salty kick combined with ripe fruit has an exhilarating effect. Lassis can be made with a variety of fruits, but papaya is one of the most popular.

2 papayas, peeled and diced

720 ml / 3 cups plain Greek yogurt (2% fat)

10 g / ½ cup fresh mint leaves

½ teaspoon freshly ground black pepper

¼ teaspoon sea salt

ice cubes, to serve

a few fresh mint sprigs, to decorate

Serves 4

Put the papaya, yogurt, mint, black pepper and salt in a blender, and add 500 ml / 2 cups cold water. Process until puréed and smooth.

Pour into 4 tall glasses filled with ice cubes. Decorate with fresh mint sprigs and serve immediately.

index

ABOUT THE CONTRIBUTORS

Pablo Uribe and **Rob Baines** own and run Snog. Pablo is Director of Product and Location Design for Snog. He set up StudioUribe in London in 1999 – an architecture and interior design studio that is involved with projects worldwide. Rob is CEO of Snog. After a career in investment banking he provided consultancy services to the catering trade and set up cafés at some of the busiest tourist attractions in England.

Mariana Velasquez is a chef, recipe developer and food stylist who has collaborated on more than 20 cookbooks throughout her career. She was selected to food style *American Grown*, by First Lady Michelle Obama, a project that took her into the White House kitchen and garden. A native of Colombia, Mariana now lives in New York. See more about her work at www.marianavelasquez.com.